Snacks

from around the world

Sue Ashworth

Heinemann
LIBRARY

H **www.heinemann.co.uk/library**
Visit our website to find out more information about **Heinemann Library** books.

To order:
☎ Phone 44 (0) 1865 888066
▤ Send a fax to 44 (0) 1865 314091
▢ Visit the Heinemann Bookshop at www.heinemann.co.uk/library to browse our catalogue and order online.

First published in Great Britain by Heinemann Library, Halley Court, Jordan Hill, Oxford OX2 8EJ, part of Harcourt Education.

Heinemann is a registered trademark of Harcourt Education Ltd.

Produced for Heinemann Library by Discovery Books Ltd.
Editorial: Helena Attlee, Geoff Barker, Nancy Dickmann and Tanvi Rai
Design: Jo Hinton-Malivoire and Rob Norridge
Illustrations: Nicholas Beresford-Davies
Cartographer: Stefan Chabluk
Picture Research: Laura Durman
Production: Séverine Ribierre

Originated by Dot Gradations Ltd.
Printed in China by WKT Company Limited

ISBN 0 431 11741 1
08 07 06 05 04
10 9 8 7 6 5 4 3 2 1

British Library Cataloguing in Publication Data
Ashworth, Sue
    Snacks from around the world. –
       (A world of recipes)
    641.5'3
A full catalogue record for this book is available from the British Library.

Acknowledgements
The Publishers would like to thank the following for permission to reproduce photographs: Jeffrey W Myers/Corbis: p5; Steve Lee: all other photographs.

Cover photographs reproduced with permission of Steve Lee.

Our thanks to Sian Davies, home economist.

Disclaimer
All the Internet addresses (URLs) given in this book were valid at the time of going to press. However, due to the dynamic nature of the Internet, some addresses may have changed, or sites may have ceased to exist since publication. While the author and publishers regret any inconvenience this may cause readers, no responsibility for any such changes can be accepted by either the author or the publishers.

Every effort has been made to contact copyright holders of any material reproduced in this book. Any omissions will be rectified in subsequent printings if notice is given to the publishers.

The paper used to print this book comes from sustainable resources.

Contents

Key

* easy

** medium

*** difficult

Words appearing in the text in bold, **like this**, are explained in the glossary.

Snacks around the world

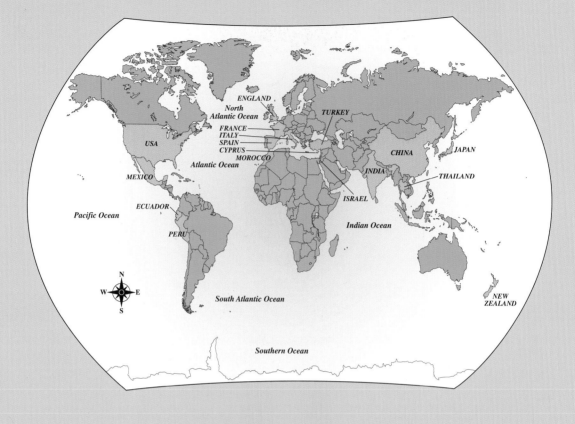

Snacks

What is a snack? It is food that we eat between meals, to give us a quick burst of energy. Sometimes we save time by eating a snack instead of a proper meal. Snacks are quick and simple to prepare and easy to eat – often you won't even need a knife and fork.

Many snacks are made from ingredients that are available locally. Sometimes they make good use of leftovers from a previous meal. For example, meat left over from a roast dinner might be used to make delicious sandwiches the next day.

All over the world people love to eat tasty snacks at different times of the day. In the UK, people may eat a sweet snack with a cup of coffee in the middle of the morning, or with tea in the afternoon. In Spain

This colourful snack bar is in Mexico City.

they eat their evening meal very late. People would get very hungry if they did not eat the **savoury** snacks called *tapas* that are served at home, or in bars and restaurants. Every country has its own favourite snacks and we have collected recipes for this book from the countries shown in yellow on the map on page 4.

Is it healthy to eat snacks?

Food is like fuel for a car. A car can't work without petrol or diesel in its tank, and you won't have any energy if you don't eat. Good food is essential for normal growth. Not all foods are good for you though. Some of them contain too much fat, salt or sugar to be healthy. The recipes in this book have been carefully chosen. Many of them contain fresh vegetables, fruit and nuts. These ingredients are all very good for you. A few of the recipes also contain starchy vegetables, like potatoes, and cereals, such as flour, oats and wheat, which will help to give your body energy.

Ingredients

potato

tortilla

pitta bread

rice

ready-made pastry

naan bread

dried apricots

garlic

dates

flaked almonds

pistachio nuts

soy sauce

Rice, bread, pastry and potatoes

Rice, bread, pastry and potatoes are all used to make delicious snacks. Rich in energy-giving **carbohydrates**, these foods also tend to be cheap, and this means that they are very suitable ingredients for snacks. Bread often forms an important part of a snack, but it may take a different form in each country. For instance, in India there are naans, while the Greeks eat pitta bread and the French have baguettes. Most countries use some kind of sandwich as a snack. Some of the recipes in this book use pastry. Both shortcrust and puff pastry can be bought ready-made, to make pies and pastries in double-quick time.

Dried fruit

Dried fruits, such as raisins, apricots or dates, make a good snack when they are eaten on their own. They are also useful ingredients for more elaborate snacks.

Nuts

Nuts are an excellent food for snacking on. They contain **protein** to help you to grow, and they are good for providing energy. There are many different varieties of nuts, and most of them can be used whole, flaked, **chopped** or even **toasted**. Nuts of all kinds make excellent snacks. Some recipes use whole or chopped nuts.

Take care though, as some people are allergic to nuts. Peanuts (also known as ground nuts) can be especially dangerous. People with nut allergies must not eat food with even the tiniest trace of nuts in it. Always check that it is all right for your guests to eat nuts and never give food containing nuts to anyone with a nut allergy.

Garlic

Garlic is often used to give its very special flavour to snacks. It is usually cooked, but it can also be used raw. Garlic is a very important ingredient in both Italian and French recipes, and there are snacks from both of these countries in this book.

Soy sauce

Soy sauce was first made in Japan and China, but now it is used all over the world. It is a rich, tasty sauce made from soya beans. In this book it is used in recipes from Japan and Thailand. In Thai recipes, *nam pla*, or fish sauce, is also a popular ingredient.

Before you start

Kitchen rules

There are a few basic rules you
should always follow when you are cooking:

- Ask an adult if you can use the kitchen.
- Some cooking processes, especially **frying**, and those using **boiling** water or syrup, can be dangerous. When you see this sign, always ask an adult for help.
- Wipe down any work surfaces before you start cooking, and then wash your hands.
- Wear an apron to protect your clothes, and tie back long hair.
- Be very careful when using sharp knives.
- Never leave pan handles sticking out, because you might knock the pan over.
- Always wear oven gloves to lift things in and out of the oven or when using a hot grill.
- Wash fruit and vegetables before you use them.

How long will it take?

Some of the recipes in this book are very quick and easy to make, while others are more difficult and may take much longer. The strip across the top of the right-hand page of each recipe tells you how long it will take to make each dish. It also shows you how difficult the dish is to make: every recipe is marked as being either * (easy), ** (medium) or *** (quite difficult). Why not start with the easier recipes?

Quantities and measurements

You can see how many people each recipe will serve by looking at the strip across the top of the right-hand page. You can multiply the quantities if you are cooking for more people, or divide them if you want to make less food, but avoid changing quantities in a **baked** dish.

Ingredients in recipes can be measured in different ways. Metric measurements use grams, litres and millilitres. Imperial measurements use ounces and fluid ounces. This book uses metric measurements. If you want to convert them into imperial measurements, use the chart on page 44.

In the recipes, you will see the following abbreviations:

tbsp = tablespoon   g = grams   cm = centimetres
tsp = teaspoon   ml = millilitres

Utensils

To cook the recipes in this book you will need these utensils (as well as essentials, such as spoons, plates and bowls):

- baking foil
- baking sheet
- **chopping** board
- draining spoon
- **fish slice**
- food processor or blender
- **grater**
- hand-held electric beaters
- jug
- kebab sticks
- kitchen paper
- large and small frying pans
- large and small saucepans
- 12-hole muffin pan

- oven gloves
- **ovenproof** dish
- pastry brush
- plain biscuit or pastry cutters
- potato **peeler**
- **serrated** knife
- set of scales
- sharp knife
- sieve
- **slotted spoon**
- **spatula**
- wire rack
- **wok**

(!) Always take great care when using kitchen knives.

Tartes à l'oignon (France)

These delicious, **savoury** tarts are fun to make. They use three ingredients that are very popular in French cookery – butter, onions and cheese (*beurre*, *oignons* and *fromage* in French). Use Cheddar cheese instead of the Brie or Camembert if you prefer.

What you need

1 sheet ready-rolled puff pastry, frozen
1 large red or white onion
1 garlic clove
25g butter
1 tsp sugar
50g Brie or Camembert

What you do

1 Take the pastry out of the freezer in advance to **thaw**. You can thaw the pastry overnight in the fridge, or you can just leave it out on a work top to thaw for about 1 hour.

2 **Preheat** the oven to 200°C/400°F/gas mark 6.

3 **Peel** the onion and garlic and **slice** them finely.

4 Melt the butter in a **frying** pan. Add the onion, garlic and sugar and cook over a gentle heat, stirring often, for about 15 minutes. The onion should be very soft and golden brown. Remove from the heat and let the mixture **cool** down a little.

5 Carefully unroll the puff pastry sheet, then use a 9-cm plain biscuit cutter to stamp out 8 circles. Place these circles on to a large **baking** sheet or two baking trays, allowing a little space between them.

6 Pile the onion mixture on top of the pastry circles, leaving a border of about 1 cm around the edge.

7 Cut the cheese into small pieces and place an equal amount on top of each little pile of onions.

(!) **8** Carefully transfer the baking sheet or trays to the oven and bake for 12–15 minutes, until the tarts have puffed up and turned golden brown. Remove from the oven. Allow the tarts to cool for a few minutes before eating.

Baked potato (England)

The English climate is perfect for growing potatoes, which are one of the country's **staple** foods. Apples grow in the orchards of the south-east, and celery is grown countrywide. Dairy cattle feed on lush pastures, giving milk to make yoghurt and cheese.

What you need

4 baking potatoes
2 celery sticks
100g Cheddar cheese
1 red apple
4 tbsp natural
   unsweetened
   yoghurt
40g butter

What you do

1 **Preheat** the oven to 200°C/400°F/gas mark 6.

2 Scrub the potatoes, then prick each one 3 or 4 times with a fork. Using an oven glove to protect your hands, carefully put the potatoes on a shelf at the top of the oven.

3 While the potatoes are **baking**, make the filling. Scrub the celery, then **chop** it into small pieces and put them into a bowl.

4 Cut the cheese into small chunks and add them to the celery in the bowl.

5 Wash the apple, **slice** it into quarters and carefully cut out the **core**. Chop the apple and add to the cheese and celery. Spoon in the yoghurt and stir everything together.

! **6** After about an hour, check that the potatoes are done by squeezing them gently – they should be slightly squashy. Remember to protect your hand by using a cloth or oven glove when you do this.

7 Slice through the middle of the potatoes and put a quarter of the butter into each one. Place on serving plates and spoon in the filling. Serve at once.

DIFFERENT FILLINGS

Try draining a can of tuna fish, mashing it with a fork and mixing in a little mayonnaise and some chopped chives to make a delicious filling. Don't forget hot baked beans with **grated** cheese for a classic favourite.

Falafel (Israel)

These spicy snacks are eaten all over the Middle East. In Egypt they are called *ta'amia* and are made from dried, white broad beans. In Israel, Syria, Lebanon and Jordan they are called *falafel*, and made from chickpeas.

What you need

2 x 400g cans chickpeas
1 red onion
2 large garlic cloves
1 small bunch of parsley
1 tsp ground coriander
1 tsp ground cumin
salt and pepper
vegetable oil, for frying
2 tomatoes
¼ cucumber
4 or 6 pitta breads

What you do

1 Drain the cans of chickpeas through a sieve, and put them into the bowl of a food processor or blender.

2 **Peel** and roughly **chop** the onion and garlic cloves. Add them to the chickpeas.

3 Chop the stalks off the parsley and throw them away. Put the leaves into the food processor with the coriander and cumin. Add some salt and pepper.

4 With an adult's help, blend the ingredients in the food processor or blender for about 20 seconds to make a smooth paste. Switch off the processor and remove the mixture, taking great care with the blade.

5 Use your hands to shape the mixture into balls, making each one about the size of a ping-pong ball. **Cover** and chill in the fridge until you want to eat.

(!) **6** Just before you are ready to eat, heat some vegetable oil in a **frying** pan and fry the falafel balls for about 5 minutes, turning them with a wooden **spatula** until golden brown. Lift them out with a **slotted spoon** and drain them on kitchen paper.

7 Chop the tomatoes and cucumber into small pieces. Mix them together in a bowl.

8 Warm the pitta bread in a **toaster** for about 1 minute. Split them open and put 2 or 3 falafel inside. Spoon in some of the tomato mixture, then serve.

Orange and almond salad (Morocco)

Oranges are grown all over Morocco, along with other citrus fruits, such as lemons and limes. Nuts, dates and grapes grow there too. This recipe combines all of these ingredients to make a delicious salad. It makes a quick, healthy snack, but it could also be served as a refreshing dessert at the end of a meal.

What you need

4 large oranges
100g seedless red grapes
100g dates
50g sultanas
25g flaked almonds
a few mint leaves

What you do

1 Using a large **chopping** board and a sharp, **serrated** knife, take a small **slice** from the top and bottom of each orange to reveal the flesh.

2 Stand an orange on the chopping board and strip the **peel** and **pith** away with the knife, working from the top of the orange to the bottom. Repeat this with the rest of the oranges.

3 Carefully cut out the segments from each orange with the knife, so that you remove all the **membrane**. Put these orange segments on to 4 plates.

4 Cut the red grapes in half, and divide the pieces between the plates.

5 Cut the dates open and remove the stones. Chop the dates into big pieces. Share these out between the plates.

6 Share out the sultanas, then **sprinkle** the almonds on top. Sprinkle each serving with a few mint leaves, then serve.

MAKING AN EFFORT

You could simply peel and divide the oranges into segments in the usual way to make this recipe, but it is worth taking the trouble to remove the pith and the membrane, as the fruit salad will be much juicier.

Empanadas (Peru)

You can buy empanadas in every market in Peru. They are little circles of pastry topped with a small mound of meat mixture, folded over and deep-fried.

What you need

6 spring onions
1 green pepper
2 garlic cloves
2 tbsp vegetable oil
250g minced pork
½ tsp mild chilli powder
1 tsp dried mixed herbs
2 tbsp tomato purée
salt and pepper
2 sheets ready-rolled shortcrust pastry

What you do

1 Wash the spring onions and **chop** them finely. Cut the pepper in half, remove the stalk, **core** and seeds and chop the flesh finely. **Peel** and chop garlic cloves.

2 Heat the oil in a large **frying** pan and add the minced pork. Fry it over a medium heat for 2–3 minutes, stirring it all the time.

3 Add the vegetables to the pork. Fry for another 3–4 minutes, stirring everything together. Turn down the heat and cook gently for 5 more minutes.

4 Stir in the chilli powder, herbs and tomato **purée**. **Season** with salt and pepper. Leave to **cool**.

5 Unroll the pastry and cut out 12 circles with a 10-cm pastry cutter. Put a little meat mixture in the middle of each circle. Dampen the edges of the circles with water, then fold the pastry over to make semi-circles. Press the edges down to seal them.

6 Grease the **baking** sheet and then arrange the empanadas on it. Using a pastry brush, **glaze** them with a little milk, and then put them in the fridge to chill.

7 **Preheat** the oven to 200°C/400°F/gas mark 6.

8 Put the empanadas in the oven and bake for about 25 minutes, or until golden brown. Cool for a few minutes. Lift them off the baking sheets with a **fish slice**. Serve warm or cold.

Grilled red peppers and halloumi (Cyprus)

Cyprus is a beautiful island in the eastern Mediterranean sea. The sun shines almost all year round, and the hot, dry climate is ideal for growing fruit and vegetables. Cyprus is famous for its halloumi and feta, cheeses made from goats' or sheep's milk.

What you need

2 large red peppers
250g halloumi cheese
2 tbsp olive oil
1 tsp dried thyme or
    mixed dried herbs
freshly ground black
    pepper

What you do

(!) **1** If you look at the top of a pepper you will see that it has lines that divide it into 6 sections. Use a knife to cut down these lines, as this is the easiest way to get 6 equal pieces. Break off the stalk end with all the seeds on it and throw it away. Run the pepper under the tap to rinse away any stray seeds that may have clung to the inside of it. Do the same with the second pepper.

2 **Preheat** the grill.

3 Arrange the pieces of pepper, skin side down, on a **baking** sheet.

4 **Slice** the block of halloumi into 12 equal pieces.

(!) **5** Grill the pieces of pepper for about 3 minutes, until they start to soften.

6 Put a slice of cheese on to each piece of pepper. **Sprinkle** with a little olive oil, then sprinkle the herbs on top. **Season** with some black pepper. (You don't need salt because the cheese is salty already).

(!) **7** Put the peppers under the grill again and cook until the cheese begins to turn brown. This will take about 2 minutes. **Cool** the peppers for a few minutes before serving.

OTHER CHEESES

Halloumi cheese is the **authentic** choice for this recipe, but you can use sliced feta cheese or sliced Cheddar instead.

Cheese muffins (New Zealand)

Muffins are often on the menu in snack bars and cafés throughout New Zealand, and are frequently cooked at home. This is a **savoury** recipe using Cheddar cheese.

What you need

vegetable oil, for greasing
250g plain flour
½ tsp salt
1 tbsp baking powder
25g caster sugar
75g Cheddar cheese
1 egg
240ml milk
90ml vegetable oil

What you do

1 **Preheat** the oven to 190°C/375°F/gas mark 5.

2 Grease a 12-hole muffin pan with vegetable oil, or use paper **baking** cups.

3 **Sift** the flour, salt and baking powder into a large mixing bowl. Stir in the sugar.

4 **Grate** the cheese, then stir it into the flour mixture.

5 Break the egg into a jug and **beat** it with a fork. Add the milk and oil and stir well.

6 Pour the egg mixture into the flour mixture. Using a metal spoon, stir until the ingredients are just combined. Do not beat this mixture or stir it too much. It will be quite lumpy, but there should be no traces of dry flour.

7 Spoon the mixture into 10 holes in the muffin pan leaving 2 holes empty. Bake for about 20 minutes, or until they have risen and turned a golden colour.

8 Cool for a few minutes, and then use a blunt knife to ease the muffins out of the tin. Muffins are best eaten on the day they are made.

Potato soup (Ecuador)

Historical evidence shows that potatoes were grown in South America thousands of years ago, long before they were a familiar vegetable in European countries. Today, many South American recipes include potatoes.

What you need

500g baking potatoes
1 large onion
2 garlic cloves
1 mild green chilli
25g butter
2 vegetable stock
   cubes
a few sprigs of fresh
   coriander
250ml milk
salt and pepper

What you do

1 **Peel** the potatoes with a potato peeler. Wash them, then cut them into small chunks.

2 Peel the onion and **chop** it finely. Peel the garlic cloves and crush them in a garlic press.

(!) 3 Cut the stalk end off the chilli and throw it away. **Slice** the chilli lengthways and remove the seeds, then chop the chilli finely. Take care that you don't rub your eyes, because the chilli will make them sting. Wash your hands with soap and water as soon as you have chopped the chilli.

(!) 4 Melt the butter in a large saucepan over a low heat. Add the onion, garlic and chilli and **fry** gently for 3–4 minutes, stirring them often.

5 Add the potatoes to the saucepan. Pour in 500ml water and crumble the stock cubes into it. Stir well. Turn up the heat until the liquid starts to **boil**, then turn the heat to low. **Simmer** gently for 40 minutes.

6 Put aside a few coriander leaves and chop the remaining coriander finely. Add it to the other ingredients in the saucepan with the milk. Heat gently until hot then **season**, **sprinkle** with remaining coriander leaves and serve at once.

Teriyaki chicken kebabs (Japan)

The main ingredient in teriyaki **marinade** is soy sauce, made from soya beans. It is a very popular Japanese flavouring that usually combines soy sauce with *mirin*, or rice wine, another well-known Japanese ingredient. It tastes excellent in this recipe, and it's a good marinade for other meat, and fish, too.

What you need

4 skinless, boneless
  chicken breasts
4 tbsp teriyaki
  marinade
1 tbsp sesame oil

What you do

1 Carefully cut the chicken into 2-cm chunks (making about 7 or 8 pieces from each chicken breast). Put them into a shallow ceramic, glass or plastic bowl, not one that is made from metal.

2 Spoon the teriyaki marinade over the chicken, then stir the chicken to coat it in the marinade. **Cover** the bowl and put it in the fridge for about 30 minutes.

3 While the chicken is in the fridge, put 10 wooden kebab sticks into a bowl of hot water. Leave them to soak. This will stop them from burning when you put them under the grill later.

4 After the chicken has been in the fridge for at least 30 minutes, **preheat** the grill.

5 Take the kebab sticks out of the water and thread the pieces of chicken on to them to make about 10 kebabs.

(!) **6** Arrange the kebabs on the grill rack and brush them with the sesame oil. Cook for about 10 minutes, turning them from time to time, taking care as you do so.

7 Lift the kebabs on to a serving plate. Let them **cool** for a couple of minutes before eating.

MAKE A MARINADE

To make your own marinade, mix together 2 tbsp of Japanese soy sauce with 2 tbsp of *mirin*, a rice wine that is available in most supermarkets.

Paprika potatoes with garlic mayonnaise (Spain)

In Spain there are lots of places where you can enjoy snacks called *tapas*. These can be made with fish, meat or vegetables. Usually there will be a bowl of garlic mayonnaise to accompany tapas – this is called *aioli*. It is delicious with crusty bread – and perfect served with these paprika-flavoured potato wedges.

What you need

4 baking potatoes
4 tbsp olive oil
2 tsp paprika
salt and pepper
6 fat garlic cloves
200g mayonnaise
150g Greek-style natural
 yoghurt
1 tbsp lemon juice

What you do

1 **Preheat** the oven to 200°C/400°F/gas mark 6.

2 Scrub the potatoes, then carefully **slice** each one in half lengthways. Put these halves flat side down, then cut each half into 4 long wedges.

3 Put all the potato wedges into a large **roasting** pan. **Sprinkle** them with the olive oil and add the paprika, salt and pepper. Now use your hands to toss the potato wedges to coat them in the **seasonings**.

4 Put the unpeeled garlic cloves in a small, **ovenproof** dish. Place in the oven, towards the top. Put the roasting dish with the potatoes on the shelf below.

(!) **5** After 25 minutes, remove the garlic from the oven, using oven gloves to protect your hands. Set to one side. Take out the potato wedges. Turn these over, using a **fish slice**, then return them to the oven for another 25 minutes.

6 When the garlic cloves have **cooled** down, squash them on a chopping board with a fork, so that the soft insides are squeezed out. Now you can throw away their papery skins. Use the fork to mash the garlic to make a paste.

7 In a bowl, mix the mayonnaise with the yoghurt and garlic paste. Season with a little salt and pepper and add the lemon juice. Stir everything together.

8 Carefully take the potato wedges out of the oven. Lift them on to serving plates with the fish slice, then serve them with the garlic mayonnaise.

Four seasons pizza (Italy)

This pizza is called *quattro stagioni* in Italian, or 'four seasons'. Each quarter of the pizza has a different topping. The pepper reminds us of spring, tomatoes mean summer, mushrooms are autumn, and the winter is represented by ham or pepperoni sausage.

What you need

1 x 23cm pizza base
2 tbsp tomato purée
2 tomatoes
75g **grated** mozzarella
   cheese
1 tsp dried, mixed
   Italian herbs
¼ red pepper
2 closed cup mushrooms
25g sliced pepperoni
   sausage

What you do

1 **Preheat** the oven to 200°C/400°F/gas mark 6.

2 Place the pizza base on a large **baking** sheet.

3 Spoon the tomato **purée** on top of the pizza base, then spread it evenly over the surface.

4 **Slice** the tomatoes thinly and then arrange them over the pizza base. Scatter most of the cheese evenly on top, then **sprinkle** with the herbs.

5 Slice the pepper. Arrange it over quarter of the pizza.

6 Slice the mushrooms thickly and arrange them over a second quarter of the pizza. Arrange the slices of pepperoni over a third quarter of the pizza. Sprinkle the rest of the cheese on top.

(!) 7 Carefully transfer the baking sheet to the oven and bake the pizza for 12–15 minutes, until the cheese is bubbling. Remove from the oven, taking care. **Cool** for a few minutes, then serve.

OTHER BASES

If you don't have pizza bases, you can make this recipe using halves of French baguette, ciabatta, or even pitta bread.

Egg fried rice (China)

Rice is a **staple** food for around half of the world's population. In China, rice has been grown in the Yangtze river valley for the last 8500 years.

What you need

250g long-grain rice
½ tsp salt
2 eggs
2 tbsp milk
6 spring onions
6 closed cup
  mushrooms
3 tbsp vegetable oil
2 tbsp soy sauce

What you do

(!) 1 Put the rice into a large saucepan and add the salt. With an adult's help, cover it with plenty of **boiling** water. Stir the rice around the pan, then cook it for 12 minutes.

(!) 2 Carefully drain the rice through a sieve, then rinse it with lots of cold water and let it drain thoroughly.

3 **Beat** the eggs and milk together in a small bowl.

4 Wash the spring onions, cut off the roots and any damaged outside leaves. **Chop** finely. Wipe the mushrooms with kitchen paper and **slice** them thinly.

(!) 5 Heat the oil in a **wok** or large **frying** pan. Add the spring onions and mushrooms and fry them for 3 minutes, stirring them often.

6 Add the eggs to the wok or frying pan and stir them around to **scramble** them. Add the rice to the pan and **stir-fry** over a medium heat for 4–5 minutes, until the rice is heated through.

7 Stir the soy sauce through the rice, ladle it into bowls and serve at once. Eat it with chopsticks if you like!

Spiced nuts (India)

This is a traditional Indian recipe for spiced nuts. The nuts make a tasty and **nutritious** snack that you can enjoy at any time of the day. If you cannot find *garam masala*, the spice mixture added towards the end of the recipe, use a medium curry powder instead.

What you need

25g butter
100g **blanched** whole almonds
100g blanched whole hazelnuts
50g shelled pistachio nuts
25g sunflower seeds
½ tsp whole cumin seeds
1 tsp salt
1 tsp *garam masala* or medium curry powder

What you do

1 **Preheat** the oven to 190°C/375°F/gas mark 5.

2 Melt the butter in a medium saucepan. Remove from the heat.

3 Put all the nuts and seeds into the saucepan. Mix them together so they are coated in the butter.

4 Tip the nut mixture on to a **baking** sheet and spread it out evenly. **Sprinkle** with the salt.

5 Carefully transfer the baking sheet to the oven. **Roast** the nuts for 8 minutes until lightly browned.

⊙ **6** Using oven gloves to protect your hands, remove the nuts from the oven and turn them over. Return to the oven for a further 7 minutes. Again, be careful when removing the baking sheet from the oven, and always use oven gloves.

7 Sprinkle the *garam masala* or curry powder over the nut mixture and stir it through. Add a little extra salt if you want to. Let the nuts **cool** down a little, and then serve them in an attractive bowl.

Quesadillas (Mexico)

These Mexican cheese turnovers are very quick to make and delicious to eat. In this recipe, the *queso* (meaning cheese) is Cheddar, though in Mexico a cheese called *queso chihuahua* is used. Here the cheese is topped with a salsa which is a mixture of finely **chopped** avocado, spring onions and tomatoes.

What you need

100g Cheddar cheese
2 large tomatoes
1 small avocado
3 spring onions
a squeeze of lemon juice
salt and pepper
vegetable oil
4 soft flour tortillas

What you do

1 **Grate** the cheese and set it to one side.

2 Chop the tomatoes into small pieces and put them into a bowl. Use a potato **peeler** to peel the avocado, and then cut it in half, around the stone. Remove the stone. Chop the flesh into small chunks and add them to the tomato.

3 Wash the spring onions, remove outer leaves and roots, and chop finely. Add them to the tomato and avocado mixture. Add a squeeze of lemon juice, then **season** the mixture with salt and pepper.

4 Grease a non-stick **frying** pan with a tiny drop of vegetable oil and put it over a medium heat.

(!) **5** Put a tortilla in the pan and **sprinkle** about a quarter of the cheese over the top. Heat for a few minutes, then sprinkle about 2 tbsp of the tomato and avocado salsa on to one half of the tortilla. Fold in half, using a wooden **spatula** or a **fish slice**. Cook for about 30 seconds, then flip the tortilla over to cook the other side for another 30 seconds, until browned on both sides.

6 Slide the cooked tortilla on to a serving plate. Continue to cook the remaining tortillas in the same way.

7 Serve the hot *quesadillas* cut into 2 or 3 pieces.

Prawn and sesame toasts (Thailand)

Fish and seafood recipes are extremely popular in Thailand, where thousands of kilometres of coastline and hundreds of inland rivers and waterways provide a plentiful supply of fresh seafood.

What you need

150g uncooked, peeled prawns
150g lean pork
3 spring onions
1 garlic clove
a few sprigs of fresh coriander
1 tbsp *nam pla* (fish sauce) or soy sauce
1 small egg
salt and pepper
6 slices thick-cut white bread
3 tbsp sesame seeds
150ml vegetable oil

What you do

1 If you are using frozen prawns, take them out of the freezer to **thaw** 45 minutes before you need them.

2 **Slice** the pork into chunks. Pat the prawns dry with kitchen paper.

3 Wash the spring onions, cut off the roots and any damaged outside leaves. **Chop** roughly. **Peel** the garlic clove.

4 With an adult's help, put the pork, prawns, spring onions, garlic, coriander sprigs and fish sauce or soy sauce into a food processor or blender. Break in the egg and **season** with salt and pepper.

5 Blend the pork and prawn mixture for about 20 seconds to make a paste. Switch off the food processor and carefully spoon the mixture out of it.

6 Cut the crusts off the bread and throw them away. Spread the mixture thickly over the slices. Now cut the bread into 4 pieces to make either 4 small squares or triangles.

7 **Sprinkle** the topping with lots of sesame seeds and press them down lightly with your fingers.

⊘ 8 Heat the vegetable oil in a **wok** or **frying** pan. Carefully put a few pieces of the bread into the wok or pan – topping side down – so that it sets and browns. Fry gently for about 2 minutes, then carefully turn over to cook the other side for another 30 seconds or so.

9 Lift out the cooked pieces with a **slotted spoon**. Drain them on sheets of kitchen paper. Fry the remaining pieces of bread. Serve hot.

Stuffed apricots and dates (Turkey)

Apricots, dates and nuts grow in Turkey, and they are often included in Turkish recipes. All of these ingredients are good for you as they provide essential **nutrients**. Both apricots and dates are good sources of fibre, which helps you to have a healthy digestive system. Nuts are a good source of **protein**, which is vital for normal, healthy growth.

What you need

12 ready-to-eat dried
  apricots
12 dried dates,
  preferably pitted
250g cream cheese
1 tbsp honey
25g unsalted pistachio
  nuts

What you do

1 Put the apricots into a heatproof bowl and cover them with **boiling** water. Leave them to soak for about 15 minutes. This will make them even more moist and delicious.

2 While the apricots are soaking remove the stones from the dates if they are not already **pitted**. To do this, carefully cut a slit along the length of each date, then use your fingers to take out the stones. They will come out quite easily.

3 Put the cream cheese into a mixing bowl and add the honey. Stir well with a wooden spoon to mix it in thoroughly.

4 Put the pistachio nuts on a **chopping** board and chop them finely.

5 Drain the apricots through a sieve, then tip them on to sheets of kitchen paper. Pat them dry.

40

6 Cut a slit in each apricot. Open up to form a little pocket, then spoon in some of the cream cheese mixture.

7 Fill the dates in the same way as the apricots.

8 Sprinkle the chopped nuts over the apricots and dates. Now they are ready to eat.

Chocolate chip cookies (USA)

You can buy chocolate chip cookies everywhere you go in the USA. There's nothing to beat home-made ones though, so here's an easy recipe for snack-sized cookies that you can make yourself.

What you need

vegetable oil, for greasing
100g butter (at room temperature)
150g light muscovado sugar
1 medium egg
½ tsp vanilla extract
150g plain flour
pinch of salt
1 tsp baking powder
75g plain chocolate drops

What you do

1 **Preheat** the oven to 180°C/350°F/gas mark 4. Grease 2 baking sheets with a little vegetable oil.

2 In a large mixing bowl, **beat** the butter and sugar together with a wooden spoon, or use hand-held electric beaters. You need to beat the mixture until it has a light, fluffy texture and is much paler in colour than it was before.

3 Beat the egg in a jug and stir in the vanilla extract, then add a little bit at a time to the creamed mixture, beating well each time.

4 Use a large sieve to **sift** in the flour, salt and baking powder. Add the chocolate drops. Stir gently together until combined.

5 Using a tablespoon, place 10 heaps of the cookie mixture on to each baking sheet. Make sure that you allow a little room for the mixture to spread out as it cooks.

6 Carefully transfer the **baking** sheets to the oven. Bake for 15–20 minutes, until the cookies are golden.

7 With an adult's help, remove the baking sheets from the oven. After a few minutes, carefully lift the cookies on to a wire rack with a **fish slice** to **cool**.

NUTTY IDEAS

If you like, add 25g of **chopped** almonds or hazelnuts to the mixture with the chocolate drops.

Further information

Here are some books and websites that will help you to find out more about snacks all over the world.

Books

The Latin American Kitchen, Elisabeth Luard (Kyle Cathie Limited, 2002).
Street Food, Clare Ferguson (Ryland, Peters & Small, 2000).
Street Food from Around the World, James Mayson (Absolute Press, 1998).

Websites

http://www.homecooking.about.com/library/index
http://www.urbanext.uiuc.edu/party/food_snacks.html

Conversion chart

Ingredients for recipes can be measured in two different ways. Metric measurements use grams and millilitres. Imperial measurements use ounces and fluid ounces. This book uses metric measurements. The chart here shows you how to convert measurements from metric to imperial.

SOLIDS		LIQUIDS	
METRIC	IMPERIAL	METRIC	IMPERIAL
10g	$\frac{1}{4}$ oz	30ml	1 fl oz
15g	$\frac{1}{2}$ oz	50ml	2 fl oz
25g	1 oz	75ml	$2\frac{1}{2}$ fl oz
50g	$1\frac{3}{4}$ oz	100ml	$3\frac{1}{2}$ fl oz
75g	$2\frac{3}{4}$ oz	125ml	4 fl oz
100g	$3\frac{1}{2}$ oz	150ml	5 fl oz
150g	5 oz	300ml	10 fl oz
250g	9 oz	600ml	20 fl oz
450g	1lb	900ml	30 fl oz

Healthy eating

This diagram shows you what foods you should eat to stay healthy. Most of your food should come from the bottom of the pyramid. Eat some of the foods from the middle every day. Only eat a little of the foods from the top.

Healthy eating is a balance of all kinds of different foods. It is fine to enjoy a sweet snack every so often, but try not to eat too many sweet things.

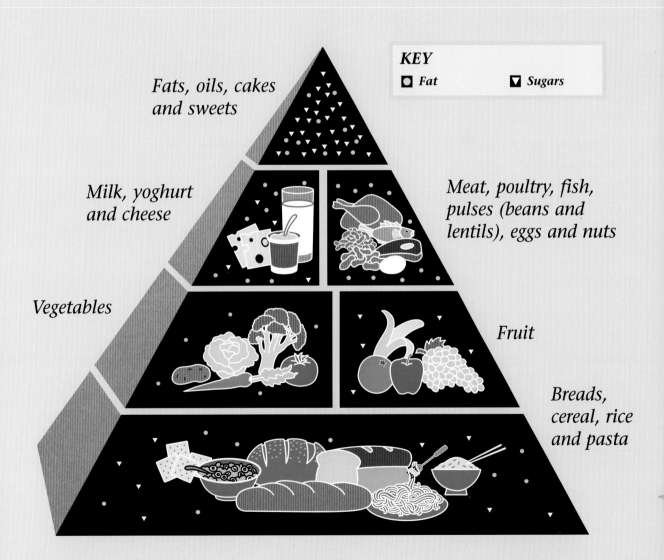

Fats, oils, cakes and sweets

KEY
☐ Fat   ▼ Sugars

Milk, yoghurt and cheese

Meat, poultry, fish, pulses (beans and lentils), eggs and nuts

Vegetables

Fruit

Breads, cereal, rice and pasta

Glossary

authentic genuine, something that comes from a particular place or country

bake cook something, such as cakes or pies, in the oven

beat mix something together strongly, using a fork, spoon or whisk

blanched made white by scalding in boiling water

boil cook a liquid on the hob (or the flat top part of a cooker). Boiling liquid bubbles and steams strongly.

carbohydrate sugary starch found in bread, potatoes, etc.

chop cut something into pieces, using a knife or blender

cool allow hot food to become cold. You should always allow food to cool before putting it in the fridge.

core hard, central part of an apple or pear, containing the seeds

cover put a lid on a pan, or foil or cling-film over a dish

fish slice flat cooking utensil, used for lifting and turning fish, but good for lifting other foods too

fry cook something in oil in a pan

glaze coat food with something to make it look glossy. This can be milk or a mixture of beaten egg and milk or sugar and water.

grate cut into small pieces, using a grater

marinade a liquid in which meat or fish can be soaked to give it more flavour

membrane thin, skin-like substance

nutrient substance in food that gives our bodies nourishment

nutritious nourishing, good for you

ovenproof will not crack in heat of oven

peel remove the skin of a fruit or vegetable; or the skin itself

pith white part of the skin of citrus fruits

pitted without stones

preheat turn the oven or grill on in advance, so that it is hot when you are ready to heat food

protein substance found in foods such as meat, eggs, cheese, fish and beans, which we need to grow and stay healthy

purée mash, sieve, liquidize or blend food until it is smooth; or the blended food itself

roast cook meat, chicken or some savoury dishes in an oven

savoury salty rather than sweet flavour

scramble cook eggs over a gentle heat until they form soft lumps

season give extra flavour to food by adding salt or pepper

serrated having tiny, sharp notches that help you to saw through foods

sift shake an ingredient, such as flour, through a sieve

simmer boil gently

slice cut something into thin, flat pieces

slotted spoon large spoon with holes in it that allows you to drain the food as you lift it

spatula flat kitchen utensil to help lift and turn things over

sprinkle scatter small pieces or drops on to something

staple one of the most important foods in a person's diet is called a staple food. Bread, rice and potatoes are staples in many countries.

stir-fry fry very fast in a large, open pan or wok

thaw defrost something that has been frozen

toast heat under a grill or in a toaster

wok a deep, curved cooking pot, mainly used for stir-frying, especially in Chinese and Southeast Asian cookery

Index